EVOLUTION
FOR
SMARTYPANTS

Anushka Ravishankar

ILLUSTRATED BY
Pia Alizé Hazarika

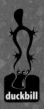

duckbill

An imprint of Penguin Random House

DUCKBILL BOOKS

USA | Canada | UK | Ireland | Australia
New Zealand | India | South Africa | China

Duckbill Books is part of the Penguin Random House group of companies
whose addresses can be found at global.penguinrandomhouse.com

Published by Penguin Random House India Pvt. Ltd
4th Floor, Capital Tower 1, MG Road,
Gurugram 122 002, Haryana, India

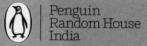
Penguin
Random House
India

First published in Duckbill Books by
Penguin Random House India 2022

Text copyright © Anushka Ravishankar 2022
Illustrations copyright © Pia Alizé Hazarika 2022

ISBN 9780143454120

Typeset in ArcherPro by DiTech Publishing Services Pvt. Ltd
Printed at Aarvee Promotions, India

www.penguin.co.in

EVOLUTION

is the process by which
a biological species changes its
characteristics over generations,
based on the natural selection
of genetic variations.

Living things give birth to other living things that are like them.

Pea plants grow from the seeds of pea plants.

Sparrows come out of sparrow eggs.

Cats give birth to cats.

Humans give birth to humans.

Each of these is a **species**.

But all pea plants are not exactly alike.
All sparrows are not exactly the same.

So there are changes within species,
which often happen for no reason.

SHORT NECK

LONG NECK

SHORT
EARS

LONG
EARS

Some of these changes are useful.

Some are not.

Suppose the birds eat seeds of the plants growing on the island. So they have small, blunt beaks which are good enough for them.

Let's call this species of birds the Bluntnosed Seedeaters.

A few of them are born with sharper beaks, but they are the odd ones. They are still Bluntnosed Seedeaters, but their beaks are sharper.

Then one summer, the plants all die and the grass dries up. There are no seeds left to eat. There are only worms, which live inside the ground.

But the birds' beaks are too small and blunt to dig into the hard ground.

The ones with the sharper beaks are able to get to the worms.

So the other birds go away to look for some island with plants and seeds, but the sharp-beaked ones stay on.

Slowly, over many, many, many years . . .

HOW MANY YEARS?

SO MANY YEARS THAT YOU CAN'T EVEN IMAGINE IT.

After many, many thousands of years, if the island remains dry, all the birds on the island will have sharper and longer beaks. This is because the birds with the short beaks will all have gone away, since they cannot get food on the island.

So the birds that remain on that island become a slightly different species, the Sharpnosed Wormeaters.

They will look different from the Bluntnosed Seedeaters. Their food will be different, too.

This slow, slow way in which one species becomes another is called **evolution.**

So, there are two steps in evolution.
The first is the changes that happen.

For example, when a Bluntnosed
Seedeater has a baby with a sharp beak,
that is a change. Such changes
happen all the time.

The second step is called the **survival of the fittest.**

NOT THAT KIND OF FITTEST!

IT MEANS FIT TO LIVE IN A PARTICULAR PLACE COMPARED TO OTHER SPECIES.

The changes that are useful, continue. For example, when the island went dry, a sharp beak was useful, so there were more and more Sharpnosed Wormeaters on the dry island. They were fit to live in a dry place, so they survived there.

This is also called **natural selection.**

It is through the natural selection of changes that the millions and billions of species on Earth began to exist.

Sometimes, one species can lead
to many different species.

Humans evolved from a kind of ape.
Monkeys, gorillas and chimpanzees also
evolved from the same kind of ape.

MONKEYS

GORILLAS

ORANGUTANS

CHIMPANZEES

NO, I'M NOT ACTUALLY A MONKEY.

Evolution also happens within one species.

Humans looked very different millions of years ago. We have evolved slowly, over many many millions of years, into what we are today.

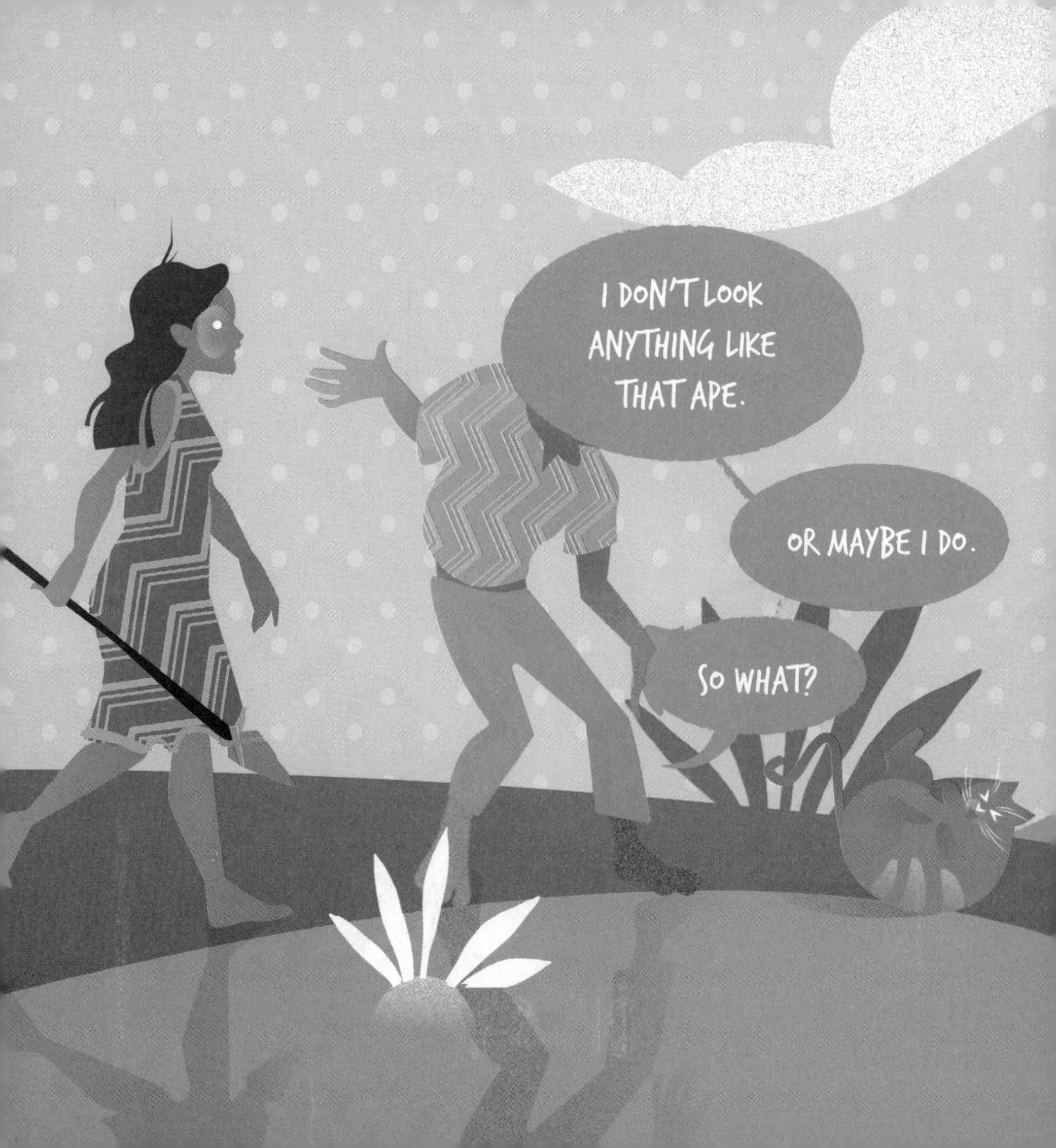
I DON'T LOOK ANYTHING LIKE THAT APE.
OR MAYBE I DO.
SO WHAT?

Cats and tigers came from the same species 10.8 million years ago!

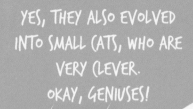

Anushka Ravishankar likes science, cats and books, not necessarily in that order. So she decided to write a book to explain science to a cat. The cat doesn't always get the point, but she hopes her readers will.

Pia Alizé Hazarika is an illustrator primarily interested in comics and visual narratives.

Her independent/collaborative work has been published by Penguin Random House India (*The PAO Anthology*), COMIX INDIA, Manta Ray Comics, The Pulpocracy, Captain Bijli Comics, Yoda Press, Zubaan Books and the Khoj Artists Collective. She runs PIG Studio, an illustration-driven space, based out of New Delhi.

Her handle on Instagram is @_PigStudio_